rstones of Freedom

The Golden Gate Bridge

SHARLENE AND TED NELSON

CHILDREN'S PRESS®
A Division of Scholastic Inc.
New York • Toronto • London • Auckland • Sydney
Mexico City • New Delhi • Hong Kong
Danbury, Connecticut

Reading Consultant: Linda Cornwell, Coordinator of School Quality and
  Professional Improvement, Indiana State Teachers Association
Content Consultant: Trubee Schock, Archives Coordinator,
  Golden Gate Bridge Highway and Transportation District

Library of Congress Cataloging-in-Publication Data

Nelson, Sharlene P.
  The Golden Gate Bridge / Sharlene and Ted Nelson.
    p. cm.—(Cornerstones of freedom)
  Includes index.
  ISBN 0-516-22025-X (lib.bdg.)   0-516-25957-1 (pbk.)
    1. Golden Gate Bridge (San Francisco, Calif.)—Juvenile literature.
  [1. Golden Gate Bridge (San Francisco, Calif.) 2. Bridges.]
  I. Nelson, Ted W. II. Title. III. Series.
  TG25.S225 N45 2001
  624'.5'0979461—dc21

00-020905

On the morning of May 27, 1937, wind blew fog through California's Golden Gate, the entrance to San Francisco Bay. Despite the cold, thousands of excited people gathered to celebrate opening day of the Golden Gate

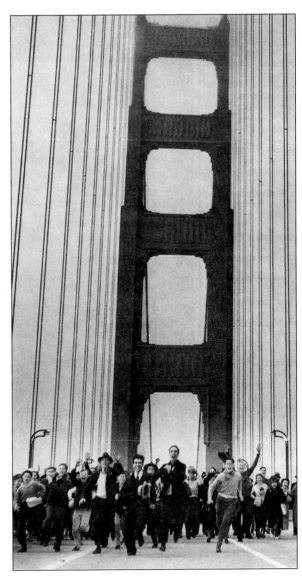

Thousands of people celebrated the opening of the Golden Gate Bridge on May 27, 1937.

Bridge. It connected the city of San Francisco on the south to Marin County on the north. The bridge was more than 1 mile (2 kilometers) long, and it was the longest suspension bridge in the world.

At 6 A.M., people began to walk, run, and dance onto the red-orange bridge. As the fog lifted, they looked up at the bridge's tall steel towers. They leaned over the railings and peered at the water far below. Some paused and listened to the wind sing through the steel cables that held the roadway in place. By the end of the day, more than two hundred thousand people had joined in the celebration.

3

The next day, police motorcycles led the first vehicles across the bridge. Then Chief Engineer Joseph B. Strauss stepped to a microphone. Strauss stood 5' 4" (163 centimeters) tall and was sixty-seven years old. Onlookers could barely hear his frail voice. It was his final speech as chief engineer. His work was done. He had created the greatest bridge of the time.

Now, more than nine million people visit the Golden Gate Bridge each year. They come to see its graceful towers. They snap pictures of San Francisco's skyscrapers, Marin County's rugged hills, and ships passing below. They walk across the bridge as cars and trucks rush by.

The Golden Gate Bridge is included as one of the "Seven Wonders of the Modern World." The bridge is also listed among the "Top 10 Construction Achievements of the 20th Century" along with New York's Empire State Building and the Panama Canal. The bridge stands because Joseph Strauss had a desire. He wanted to build the bridge that many said, "couldn't be built."

Joseph Strauss was born on January 7, 1870. While growing up in Cincinnati, Ohio, he dreamed of achieving great works. He wrote poetry and tinkered in a machine shop inventing gadgets. As an engineering student at the University of Cincinnati, he was chosen class poet. At graduation ceremonies in 1892, he

stunned his professors by describing his design for a 50-mile (80-km)-long bridge across the Bering Strait connecting Alaska and Russia.

For a time, Strauss worked at a Chicago bridge building company. There he proposed a new design for bridges used over narrow waterways. The company's engineers rejected his idea. He quit, rented an office, and started his own bridge building company in 1902.

In 1917, Strauss was in San Francisco to build a bridge over a small, city waterway. While he was there, he visited Michael M. O'Shaughnessy, San Francisco's City Engineer.

At the time, many people talked about building a bridge across the Golden Gate. O'Shaughnessy liked to ask engineers what they thought about the idea. One day, he asked Strauss. Then O'Shaughnessy added, "Everybody says it can't be done and that it would cost [$100 million] if it could be done."

Left: Joseph B. Strauss devoted twenty years of his life to building the Golden Gate Bridge.

Right: Michael M. O'Shaughnessy, San Francisco's City Engineer

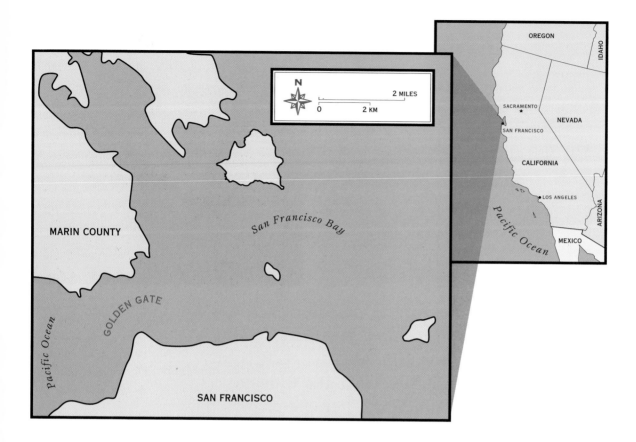

The Golden Gate is a water gap that separates the city of San Francisco and Marin County.

The Golden Gate is a narrow gap where the waters of the Pacific Ocean meet the waters of San Francisco Bay, one of the world's great harbors. A bridge across the Golden Gate would have to be high enough for the tallest ships to sail beneath. It would have to be more than 1 mile (2 km) long. It would have to be built in swift currents. It would have to withstand earthquakes and fierce winds. No one had ever built a bridge in a place like this.

Still, a bridge was needed. San Francisco is surrounded by water on three sides. In the early 1900s, San Francisco was the only city in the United States where most people traveled to and

6

from by ferry. Many of these people came from Marin County and other counties to the north.

The ferries were crowded, and people grumbled. On one holiday, cars were lined up 7 miles (11 km) at a Marin County dock waiting for a ferry to San Francisco. The last car finally reached San Francisco two days later!

Challenged by O'Shaughnessy's question, Strauss later hiked to a hill overlooking the Golden Gate. As he watched the waves break against the shores, he knew it would be a difficult bridge to build. But, the setting of sea and hills inspired him. Strauss had already built four hundred bridges, though none as grand as a Golden Gate bridge. He decided that he would build it.

Strauss told O'Shaughnessy that he could span the Gate for far less than $100 million. Strauss returned to his office in Chicago and began working on a design. On June 28, 1921, he gave his design for a Golden Gate bridge to O'Shaughnessy. The design showed two massive towers with steel framework supporting the roadway at each end. Cables supported the roadway at the bridge's center.

Strauss submitted this design for the Golden Gate Bridge in 1921.

Now Strauss needed to promote his bridge. "The value of an idea," he once said, "depends not only on the sweat you put into thinking it up, but also on the sweat you put into getting people to accept it." Strauss gave speeches to citizen groups and community leaders. He told audiences that his bridge would be the largest in the world. It would cost $20 million and could be completed in 1927. He said driving across the bridge would be faster and easier than riding ferries. San Francisco and the communities across the Golden Gate would prosper.

In 1923, the state of California passed a law creating the Golden Gate Bridge and Highway District. The law allowed San Francisco and the northern counties to borrow money to build the bridge. The money would be repaid by bridge tolls. Strauss's dream seemed close to reality.

Then people began to oppose the idea. Some engineers said the bridge would cost $112 million. One engineer said the rock to support the towers was weak like "plum pudding." When Strauss said he designed the bridge to sway in earthquakes and strong winds, an official called it a "rubber bridge." Lawsuits were filed to stop construction.

In speeches and in the courts, Strauss battled his opponents. Finally, he won. In 1932, the Bank of America agreed to loan the Golden Gate Bridge and Highway District the money to build the bridge. In the 1930s, the United States was in the midst of the Great Depression. Jobs were scarce, and people were eager to go to work.

On January 5, 1933, construction began on a bridge that would look nothing like the one that Strauss originally designed. During the long delays, Strauss hired Charles A. Ellis, a brilliant engineer, and Irving F. Morrow, an architect. Ellis and Morrow created a new design using new bridge building technology. Their design was a beautiful, suspension bridge with two tall towers and a roadway supported by steel cables. It was as though Strauss's design was a caterpillar from which Ellis and Morrow created a butterfly.

A 1931 drawing by architect Irving Morrow shows the bridge's final design.

Crews began to work on the anchorages at each end of the bridge. The anchorages were heavy blocks of concrete that would hold the ends of suspension cables in place. At each anchorage, pits large enough to hold a twelve-story building were carved out of the rocky ground. Dynamite blasted the rock, and steam shovels dug out the rubble.

Workers smoothed layer after layer of concrete to build the anchorages.

"A river of concrete," as one worker said, began to fill the pits. Mixer trucks delivered the concrete made from crushed oyster shells, water, and gravel. Then the concrete was poured through long hoses called "elephant trunks" to workers in the pits. They wore high rubber boots and packed and leveled the concrete inside wooden forms.

Steel eyebars that looked like giant needles were set in the concrete at each anchorage. Later, the wires of the suspension cables would be attached to the eyebars. While crews worked on the anchorages, others worked on the two piers. The piers would support the bridge's towers.

Beneath the cliffs of the Marin County shore, workers built a temporary dam. The dam was built with wood, rock, and metal plates and shaped like a horseshoe. The dam's closed end was in the water, and the open side butted

In this photograph, the steel eyebars are sticking out of a concrete anchorage. The eyebars would later hold the ends of the two suspension cables.

against the cliffs. When the water within the dam was pumped out, bass and cod flopped about on the wet rocks. Workers eagerly scooped up the fish to take home for dinner.

Inside the dam, a pit was dug and concrete was poured into wooden forms. When the dam was removed, the top of the pier was 44 feet (13 meters) above the water's surface. By midsummer 1933, Strauss could see the Marin pier from the window of his San Francisco apartment.

The Marin pier was the first major part of the Golden Gate Bridge to be completed. The dam around the pier was later removed.

The Marin pier was completed two months ahead of schedule, but the crews working on the San Francisco pier struggled. This pier had to be built 1,100 feet (335 m) from the shore, in swift currents where waves rolled in from the Pacific. Strauss and his engineers designed a trestle, a temporary steel-and-wood structure, so workers and equipment could travel across the water to the pier site.

After eight months of work, a ship lost in the fog rammed the nearly finished trestle. The damage was repaired. A few months later, storm waves tore through the trestle. More than half its length had to be rebuilt.

In the meantime, crews worked from a barge anchored over the San Francisco pier site. They were digging a pit in the Golden Gate's hard, rock bottom for the foundation of the pier and a fender. The fender, a ring of concrete designed by Strauss, would protect workers from waves and currents while they built the pier. The fender would later shield the pier from ship collisions.

As the barge pitched and rolled in the waves, the often seasick men dropped a heavy steel bar through a pipe to the rock below. The bar chipped a hole in the rock. Then small bombs followed. On impact, they exploded and enlarged the hole. After crews made a series of holes, they lowered larger bombs, and divers went to work.

The divers could be in the water only about twenty minutes at a time, four times per day, when the currents were weak between high and low tides. Even then, said one diver, "While it [the current] was slowing down or speeding up, it could still move fast enough to come awhipping in and knock you for a loop."

Groping about in the dark water, the divers retrieved wires attached to the large bombs. They brought the wires to the barge, and the crew connected them to a firing mechanism. The barge was pulled away, and the bombs were set off. After the explosion, the barge was pulled back, and a crane lifted the rubble to another barge for dumping at sea. The process was repeated again and again until the underwater pit was the size of a football stadium. At its deepest part, the pit's bottom was 110 feet (34 m) below the water's surface.

The San Francisco pier and its fender had to be built at the end of a long trestle where men on a barge dug a deep, underwater pit.

Divers worked underwater to help build the San Francisco fender and pier.

The trestle was completed in March 1934. Cranes at the trestle's end began lowering wood and steel forms, and divers positioned them in the pit. Concrete was poured into the forms. Form by form and pour by pour, the fender took shape. The fender was completed in October, and it looked like a giant bathtub. The fender was filled with concrete to about two-thirds of its height. The water inside was pumped out, and men started to build the San Francisco pier.

While work was progressing on the trestle and fender, the Marin tower was slowly rising skyward. Cranes that looked like giant spiders lifted steel sections and stacked them together and on top of each other to build the tower's legs. As the tower grew taller, pulleys and wire ropes pulled the cranes higher.

Cranes lifted steel sections to build the Marin tower.

The boxlike sections of the tower weighed an average of 45 tons (41 metric tons). These sections had hundreds of holes for rivets—metal pins used to fasten two pieces of material together. When the holes of two sections were aligned, workers crawled inside to fasten the sections together.

On platforms outside the sections, workers heated rivets in the coals of a forge. The white-hot rivets were sent through tubes to the men inside. Using tongs, they slipped the nearly molten rivets into the holes and held them in place with an iron bar. A worker in the adjoining section rounded the rivets' heads with a clattering air hammer. When the rivets cooled, they formed a solid bond between the sections.

Men wearing leather hard hats climbed around and inside the tower's steel sections to rivet them together.

Inside the sections, the crews used head-lights to see their work. They scrambled about on narrow ladders. In these cramped spaces, they breathed fumes given off when the hot rivets touched the steel covered with lead paint. Many became sick from lead poisoning. Some lost their hair and teeth. Strauss ordered them to wear respirator masks, and he had fresh air pumped into the sections. He then ordered crews to apply lead-free paint to the new sections.

Although some workers encountered these hazards on the tower, everyone on the bridge braved the weather. One man said, "It was cold and windy, and the wind would cut right through you." To help keep warm, a few wrapped themselves in newspapers and then pulled on their sweaters, overalls, and coats. "You wondered how you could move," he added. "And, your feet were still frozen."

The weather also affected the bridge's steel. As the Marin tower was being built, wind-driven salt air began to corrode its metal. Painters began to brush the steel with a first coat of reddish, protective paint. Later, officials argued about the bridge's final color. Some wanted silver, gray, or even black. Strauss and architect Morrow wanted to use "International Orange," a red-orange color. They said this color would enhance the bridge's appearance against the

greens and golds of the hills and the blues of the water and sky. Their color was chosen.

The Marin tower was completed in October 1934. Six hundred thousand rivets held the tower's legs together. Now, people around the bay began to share Strauss's vision of his bridge. The tower was tapered, with more sections at the base than at the top. This design made the tower appear taller than it really was. Decorative panels, designed by Morrow, covered the bracing between the tower's legs above where the roadway would be. The openings between the panels looked like windows to the sky.

Painters began brushing the first coat of paint on the Marin tower before it was completed.

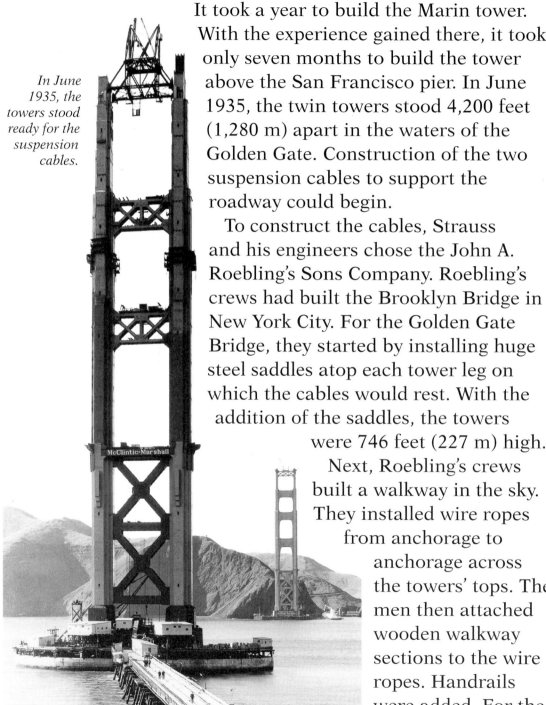

It took a year to build the Marin tower. With the experience gained there, it took only seven months to build the tower above the San Francisco pier. In June 1935, the twin towers stood 4,200 feet (1,280 m) apart in the waters of the Golden Gate. Construction of the two suspension cables to support the roadway could begin.

To construct the cables, Strauss and his engineers chose the John A. Roebling's Sons Company. Roebling's crews had built the Brooklyn Bridge in New York City. For the Golden Gate Bridge, they started by installing huge steel saddles atop each tower leg on which the cables would rest. With the addition of the saddles, the towers were 746 feet (227 m) high. Next, Roebling's crews built a walkway in the sky. They installed wire ropes from anchorage to anchorage across the towers' tops. The men then attached wooden walkway sections to the wire ropes. Handrails were added. For the

Workers built wooden walkways connecting the towers' legs and the anchorages so the cable spinners had a place to work.

first time, workers could walk across the Golden Gate! Now, the cable spinners—men who would build the cables—had a place to work.

At each anchorage, the spinners unreeled wire as thin as a drinking straw from large spools and looped it onto spinning wheels. The wheels were mounted on carriages that were pulled along by wire ropes above the walkways. Pulling loop after loop between the anchorages, the carriages and wheels moved at 650 feet (198 m) per minute. The spinners worked as winds blew and the walkways swayed back and forth. To warm up, they huddled briefly in warming shacks.

Spinning wheels pulled loops of wire across the Golden Gate. Cable spinners laid the wires into saddles atop each tower leg.

As work progressed, more spinning wheels were added to the carriages. Then 1,000 miles (1,600 km) of wire were carried daily across the Golden Gate. Each suspension cable was spun with 40,000 miles (64,372 km) of wire. There were more than twenty-seven thousand wires in each cable. The cable spinners bundled these wires into sixty-one strands and attached them to the eyebars at each anchorage. The cable spinners completed their job on May 20, 1936, nearly two months ahead of schedule. They celebrated for three days!

After the celebration, Roebling's crews used a specially designed machine and squeezed the strands of each cable into a circular form. Each cable, more than 3 feet (1 m) thick, was ready for wire rope suspenders. The crews hung suspenders at intervals along the cables. The suspender ends dangled in the wind until the roadway crews reached them.

In late summer of 1936, barges began to deliver the roadway's steel to the base of the towers. Cranes lifted the steel to the roadway level. Box-shaped beams were attached to the suspenders to form the outside of the 90-feet (27-m)-wide roadway. Different lengths and shapes of steel were lowered into place to form the roadway's framework.

As ships passed below, workers built the roadway's steel framework.

The roadway was built in opposite directions away from each tower to keep an even strain on the suspension cables.

For the crews on the roadway, every day was like working at the edge of a cliff. In wind, rain, and fog they walked along the steel, attaching each piece into place. One slip and they would fall more than 200 feet (61 m) to the water below. Bridge builders had a saying that for every $1 million spent to build a bridge, there would be one accidental death. The Golden Gate Bridge would eventually cost $35 million.

Thirty-five accidental deaths were not acceptable to Strauss. From the beginning, he required every worker to wear a leather hard hat as protection against falling objects. When work on the roadway began, Strauss ordered a net suspended beneath the workers. This was the first time a safety net was used in bridge building. Nineteen men fell into the net and were saved.

In November 1936, Strauss climbed onto one of the roadway cranes. Officials from San Francisco and the northern counties watched as Strauss lowered a beam into place. The final gap in the bridge was filled. The bridge's design was so exact that the ceremony was timed for the afternoon sun to warm and expand the steel to give it a perfect fit. The placing of this piece of steel signaled that Strauss's work as the bridge's chief engineer was almost done.

As work on the roadway neared completion, men—looking like spiders on a web—painted the wire rope suspenders.

23

When the rest of the roadway's steel framework was in place, crews formed a mat for the roadway's concrete. Temporary wooden forms were built to hold the concrete.

In three and one-half years of construction, only one accidental death had occurred. Then, on February 17, 1937, just three months before the bridge was finished, Strauss's worst fears came true. A platform beneath the roadway broke loose and plunged through the safety net. Twelve men fell to the water. Ten were lost. Two were rescued by a fishing boat. Two men had grabbed a beam and clung to it, their feet dangling in the air. They were pulled to safety. One had been smoking a pipe, and he still held it tightly between his teeth.

Work was stopped for the day. Later, the net was repaired, and crews completed the roadway and the bridge's approaches. The approaches were highways built to connect the bridge with streets and roads on each side.

Opening day drew closer. Roebling's crews wrapped the suspension cables with thin wire and removed the wooden walkways. Men cleared the bridge of construction debris. Painters continued to work.

Along the sidewalks, crews installed handrails and lights designed by architect Morrow. The handrail supports were spaced so motorists could see the ocean and bay.

The lights cast a soft, yellow glow to help motorists see in the fog. On clear nights, the lights looked like a necklace across the Golden Gate.

As opening day neared, Boy Scouts and Girl Scouts planted orange poppies and blue lupines at the bridge's entrances. Bronze plaques were mounted on the San Francisco side to honor the bridge planners and the eleven men who died in its construction. The governors of twelve western states and officials in Canada and Mexico received invitations to the event. Flags flew along the streets of San Francisco. Fireworks were set in place.

Painters put the finishing touches on the suspension cables and the handrails.

The statue of Joseph Strauss stands near the San Francisco entrance to the Golden Gate Bridge.

On May 27, 1937, bridge workers and their families joined the thousands who walked and skipped on the bridge. The workers knew the bridge was special. One worker later said, "I'm sure that any man that ever had anything to do with the bridge thought of it as his bridge." After the celebrations, Joseph Strauss quietly retired. Nearly a year later, he died of a heart attack.

Among the people who visit the Golden Gate Bridge each year are thousands of school-children. Near the place where the scouts planted the poppies and lupines, the children and other visitors gaze at a statue of Joseph Strauss. It honors the man who once said, "Our world today revolves around things which at one time couldn't be done. Don't be afraid to dream."

Joseph Strauss's dream was to build a bridge that many said couldn't be built.

FUN FACTS ABOUT THE

- The Golden Gate was given its name in 1846 by the American explorer John C. Frémont. He foresaw the time when ships carrying riches from around the world would pass through the entrance to San Francisco Bay.

- The Golden Gate Bridge is a suspension bridge. Its main span is 4,200 feet (1,280 m) long. The two side spans are 1,125 feet (343 m) long. The towers are 746 feet (227 m) high. The roadway is 220 feet (67 m) above the water. Each suspension cable is made with 40,000 miles (64,372 km) of wire.

- When completed, the Golden Gate Bridge was the longest suspension bridge in the world. Now there are six suspension bridges that are longer. They are: New York's Verrazano-Narrows Bridge, two bridges in Europe, two in China, and the world's longest—the Akashi-Kaikyo Bridge—near Kobe, Japan. Built in 1998, its main span is 6,532 feet (1,991 m) long.

- In its first year, more than three million vehicles crossed the Golden Gate Bridge. The toll was fifty cents each way. Now, more than three and one-half million vehicles cross the bridge every month, and the toll is $3 for southbound vehicles only. Since it opened, the bridge has carried more than one and one-half billion vehicles. More than one billion dollars have been collected in tolls.

- Drivers have found different ways to pay the toll. One had his pet chimpanzee give the money to the toll collector. A motorcyclist paid with money held between his teeth. When one motorist couldn't afford the toll, an alert toll collector saw that the car was being driven without keys. The motorist had used wires to steal the car. The toll collector called the police, and the driver was arrested.

GOLDEN GATE BRIDGE

- More than two hundred people work for the Bridge Division of the Golden Gate Bridge, Highway and Transportation District. Among them are toll collectors, security officers, tow-truck drivers, gardeners, ironworkers, painters, and engineers.

- Working year round, ironworkers replace corroded rivets, and painters repaint corroding surfaces. They ride up the towers in elevators. Engineers design and direct major repairs. In the 1970s, new suspender cables were installed, and in the 1980s the concrete roadway was replaced.

- In December 1951, the bridge was closed to traffic due to high winds. The roadway was strengthened after the storm. Since then, the bridge has been closed only twice by high winds.

- On a morning in May 1987, the bridge was closed to traffic. Nearly 300,000 people crowded onto the bridge to celebrate its fiftieth annivesary.

- The bridge has survived many earthquakes without damage. But, after a severe earthquake in 1989, plans were made to strengthen the bridge and the approaches against future quakes. The work will take many years and cost several times the bridge's original cost.

- Visitors to the bridge can park on the north or south side. From there, they walk or ride bicycles along the roadway's sidewalks. Walkers have the right of way, and skateboards, in-line skates, and roller skates are not allowed. Visitors to the Golden Gate Bridge web site reach it at this address:

www.goldengate.org

A "School Projects" link gives facts about the bridge and its history.

GLOSSARY

air hammer – a handheld tool that uses compressed air to strike an object with great force

anchorage – a heavy block of concrete that holds the ends of suspension cables in place

architect – a person who designs structures

barge – a broad, flat-bottomed boat pushed and pulled by tugboats

beam – a long, heavy piece of wood or metal used as a main horizontal support of a structure

cable – a thick, strong rope made of wire

corrode – to wear away gradually

crane – a machine that raises and lowers heavy weights with a swinging arm

Workers on barges dug an underwater pit to build the San Francisco pier.

engineer – a person who has been trained to design, build, or operate useful things. Civil and structural engineers usually work on bridges.

fender – a ring of concrete designed so crews would have a dry place to work and be protected from waves and currents

forge – a furnace where metal is heated

framework – a basic supporting part or structure

pier – a support for a bridge

rivet – a metal pin used to fasten two pieces of material together

suspension bridge – a bridge with the roadway supported by two overhead cables that pass over towers and are anchored at each end. There is a main span between the towers and shorter, side spans between the towers and the anchorages.

technology – a known way to make useful things or to achieve a useful purpose

Riveting the tower's steel sections together

tongs – long-handled pliers for picking up objects

trestle – a temporary steel-and-wood structure designed so workers and equipment could travel across water

TIMELINE

1870 *January 7:* Joseph B. Strauss born

Strauss starts his bridge building company **1902**

June 28: Strauss submits first design for **1921** Golden Gate Bridge

1923 California legislature creates Golden Gate Bridge and Highway District; objections to bridge cause delays

1932 Money is loaned to build bridge

1933

October: Marin **1934** tower completed

October 28: San **1935** *January 8:* San Francisco pier completed; Francisco fender *June 28:* San Francisco tower completed completed **1936** *May 20:* Spinning of suspension cables completed *December 14:* All roadway steel in place

January 5: Bridge construction begins

June 29: Marin pier completed

1937

February 17: Ten men killed in fall through safety net

May 16: Joseph Strauss dies of a **1938** heart attack

April 15: All roadway concrete paving completed

May 27, 28: Golden Gate Bridge opens

INDEX (**Boldface** page numbers indicate illustrations.)

PHOTO CREDITS

Photographs ©: Ben Davidson: 26; California Historical Society: 5 right (FN-26663, La Fayette, San Francisco), 20 (FN-23529, Piggott Photographs, San Francisco), 25 (FN-26834); Golden Gate Bridge, Highway and Transportation District: 17 (George Douglas), 22 (Charles M. Hiller), 5 left, 7, 11, 13, 19, 23, 30 top, 31 top left, 31 top right; Liaison Agency, Inc.: 1 (Michael J. Howell), cover (Wolfgang Kaehler), 28, 29 (Mark Lewis), 2, 27 (Ronald William May); Moulin Archives, S.F.: 9, 10, 14, 15, 18, 21, 30 bottom, 31 bottom left; *The San Francisco Examiner:* 3, 31 bottom right.

Maps by TJS Design, Inc.

PHOTO IDENTIFICATIONS

Cover: This daytime view of the Golden Gate Bridge shows the Marin County side of the bridge.
Page 1: This nighttime view of the Golden Gate Bridge shows the San Francisco side of the bridge.
Page 2: This close-up shows one of the bridge's towers and its suspension and suspender cables.

ABOUT THE AUTHORS

Sharlene and Ted Nelson grew up in California. As a boy, Ted watched the building of the Golden Gate Bridge from his San Francisco home. The couple now lives near Seattle, Washington. Their books include guides to West Coast lighthouses and sailing on the Columbia River. For children, they have written about national parks, logging in the old west, and biographies of famous people.